To my closest friends, who inspired this book:
Evelyn & Ethan Scott, Faith & Cole Perlick, and Addison & Cooper Ray

BUILDING INTENTIONAL RELATIONSHIPS

The Secret to Genuine Connection

SARAH MEHESY

Paperback ISBN 978-1-960007-82-7
eBook ISBN 978-1-960007-83-4

Published by

Orison Publishers, Inc.
PO Box 188
Grantham, PA 17027
www.OrisonPublishers.com

Contents

Preface

My purpose in writing this book is to help you become more intentional in your relationships with others, both personal and professional. When it comes to your professional relationships and networking, I hope the word *networking* will stop being something you wince at or a chore you dread, and you will instead enjoy the process and even be excited about it. When you define networking as *building mutually beneficial relationships*, it changes the game. You are now building genuine and authentic relationships that are not transactional but benefit both of you.

I also want to discuss what it means to intentionally build deep and meaningful personal relationships. How do we make friends and keep them? How do we stay intentional and not take them for granted? How do we know once we have built an amazing friendship? I will discuss how to make friends and keep them and share some stories along the way.

It might be helpful to define some terms I use frequently in this book. The first is *intentional*. This book is about how to build intentional relationships. What does *intention* mean? In his book *Unreasonable Hospitality*, Will Guidara defines it this way: "Intention means every decision, from the most obviously significant to the seemingly mundane, matters. To do something with intentionality means to do it thoughtfully, with clear purpose and an eye on the desired result."[1]

When I read his book and discovered this definition, I thought it was perfect. To do something with intention means that every decision I make matters. Whether big or small, it must be done with an eye on my purpose and the desired result. This is the definition I want you to think of every time you read the word *intention* in this book. Highlight it, refer to it, and come back to this definition and the two other words I am about to define.

---

1 Will Guidara, *Unreasonable Hospitality* (Penguin Random House, 2022), p. 22.

The next word that I frequently use in this book is *authenticity*. We hear this term so often— "People won't like you unless you're *yourself*" or "It's so important to be *authentic*"—that the word sometimes loses its meaning. We know *generally* what people mean by it, but it can be hard to put our fingers on what they *actually* mean. In her book, *The Gifts of Imperfection*, Brené Brown, who has studied and written about shame, empathy, courage, and vulnerability, defines authenticity as follows:

> Authenticity is the daily practice of letting go of who we think we're supposed to be and embracing who we are. Choosing authenticity means cultivating the courage to be imperfect, to set boundaries, and to allow ourselves to be vulnerable; exercising the compassion that comes from knowing that we are all made of strength and struggle; and nurturing the connection and sense of belonging that can only happen when we believe that we are enough.[2]

Being authentic means letting go of trying to be someone others want us to be and instead, being who we are. It is so important to be authentic in every relationship we have. If we cannot be authentic, we are not being ourselves, which is a problem. While I understand this is easier said than done, it is very important that we strive toward authenticity. Ask yourself: Can I be authentic in this relationship? Can I let go of who I think I should be and embrace who I am? If you do not feel safe or comfortable being authentic in some of your relationships, ask yourself why this is. Maybe it is a sign you need to reexamine some of your relationships, because if you don't feel safe being yourself, you should not be friends with someone. It's normal for it to take a little time for you to feel comfortable and safe with someone, but if it's been months or years and you still don't feel safe to be authentic, it is a sign that maybe you need to look for a new friendship.

Lastly, I want to define the phrase *being present*. Like *authenticity*, the word *present* is overused in our culture. "It's important to always be present" or "Don't worry about tomorrow; be present today." While we might not like to admit it, being present is hard—especially when our minds are constantly running. We get so busy that we struggle to pause and *be present* in relationships. Guidara writes: "I often describe 'being present' as caring so much about what you're doing that you stop caring about everything else you need to do next."[3]

When I heard that definition in Guidara's book, I realized "being present" is what I have struggled with most. Being "in the moment" can be very

---

2 Brené Brown, *The Gifts of Imperfection*, (Hazelden Publishing, 2010), p. 68.
3 Guidara, *Unreasonable Hospitality*, p. 183.

hard for me. My mind is always running, and I struggle to relax. Every time I try to sit down and take a break from being productive, my mind is buzzing, telling me I should be using my time differently.

Guidara's definition of being present has changed my relationships. Now, before a business meeting, I remind myself to take a breath and stop thinking about my to-do list. What being present looks like in practice is listening actively to whomever I'm conversing with and asking good questions. When I meet with my friends, I clear my mind and focus on our conversations. I want each person in my life to have my full attention when we are talking. Wrangling my mind in this way is easy in concept, deceptively hard in practice, and well worth the effort, because it yields strong friendships and business relationships

PART 1

Building Intentional Relationships in Business

CHAPTER 1
Intentional Relationships

There are two schools of thought when it comes to building intentional relationships. One is that relationships need to be fifty-fifty, meaning you and your colleague both have to initiate get-togethers. The other is that you will initiate contact with the people whom you want to keep in your life, regardless of how often they initiate meetings. The majority of people believe in the first school of thought. I, however, am a bigger fan of the second school of thought.

Here's the problem. When you think a relationship needs to be fifty-fifty, you keep this scorecard in your head. You compare yourself with your colleague and look at your text messages to see how often you initiated conversations versus how often the other person has. The other problem with this way of thinking is that you will lose the relationship if the other person does not initiate to the degree you deem acceptable. While you might not think you think this way, you probably do. Most people do. It's the way I was raised to think about relationships.

Now, don't get me wrong; relationships need to be mutual. Both people must want to be in the relationship for it to work. That is obvious. However, you can have a mutual relationship even if the scorecard is lopsided—and even if you initiate contact most or all of the time. You might be wondering how this is so. I understand. We are conditioned to think that the scorecard needs to be even, and that the other person should initiate contact as often as you do for the relationship to be mutual.

My definition of a *mutual* relationship is different from other people's. When I evaluate that aspect of a relationship, I ask myself the following questions.

Mutual Relationship Questions

1. Do they intentionally make time for you despite their busy schedule?
2. Do they value your time and appreciate your intentionality in connecting with them?
3. Do they express an enjoyment and appreciation of the friendship and a desire to continue it?
4. Have you made an equal mental and emotional investment in each other?
5. Is there a mutual give and take in the friendship, in talking, listening, and giving advice?

If the answers to these questions are yes, then it is a mutual relationship. This is how I view my business relationships. In some of those relationships, we both initiate. In others, I am the primary one to initiate; and sometimes I am the only one to initiate. Regardless of how much someone initiates, I will still initiate and meet with that person as long as the relationship is mutual. I choose whom I want to keep in my life and whom I don't. And so do you. These are conscious choices, whether we realize it or not. When we stop keeping score and decide that as long as the relationship is mutual, we will continue it, it frees us from comparison, prevents us from dropping potentially good relationships, and allows us to intentionally choose who to keep in our lives and which relationships to let go of.

Think about it. When you were growing up, the people you spent the most time with were usually the ones who stayed in your life. The people you didn't spend time with eventually left. Sometimes, this can happen intentionally, and sometimes it occurs unintentionally. But it happens. Once you agree that as long as a relationship is mutual, you don't care about the scorecard or how often you each initiate, it frees you up to be incredibly intentional in your relationship with that person. Have you ever thought, *I wish that one person was still in my life, but we lost touch*? If we are intentional in our relationships, then we are the ones to choose who stays in our lives and who goes.

If you still don't believe you can let go of the scorecard and the need for mutual initiation, consider this: People I have known who hold the view that the scorecard needs to be "even" eventually lose many or all of their contacts. If you don't see your colleagues, eventually, they are no longer colleagues. Letting go of this viewpoint frees us to be incredibly intentional in our relationships.

The Relationship Check-In

You might agree with this viewpoint but are unsure of how to know if a relationship is mutual if you are the only one initiating. In addition to asking yourself the questions above, consider doing a relationship check-in. What is this? It is where you check in with your colleagues—or your friends—to see if they still value the relationship and want to continue it. Doing this might sound like it would come across as weird or awkward, but it doesn't have to be.

I will share a story about someone I did a relationship check-in with. This person is one of my closest friends, and I answered yes to all of the mutual-relationship questions about them. They make time for me, value my time, and appreciate my intentionality in connecting with them. They express enjoyment and appreciation of the friendship and a desire to continue it. But I only know they desire to continue it *because I asked*.

So the story is this. I was catching up with a friend who always leaves the initiating to me. Toward the end of our meeting, I said, "Hey, I want to let you know that I appreciate and value our friendship. I know we don't get to meet up as often as we wish we could, but I would really like to continue to stay connected with you no matter where we end up in life." Then my friend said, "Thanks, I feel the same exact way. I really value your friendship because you are one of my closest friends, and I definitely want to stay connected with you as well."

That is how you do a relationship check-in. It isn't hard, weird, or awkward. It is good to do it every once in a while, especially with people who never or seldom initiate. Another thing we don't always think about is where people are with their mental health. Sometimes, people are struggling or are not in a place to reach out and need you to be the intentional one for a season. When I have been down, struggling with motivation, or very busy, I have had to physically force myself to be intentional, which I seldom have to do because I am naturally extroverted. So, think about how much harder it would be for someone struggling with anxiety or depression when they withdraw and stop going out.

Making Sure There Is Equal Investment

If your colleague or friend is not equally invested in the relationship, you will probably know without needing to do a relationship check-in. If you go back to the mutual-relationship questions, you will find that the answer to one or several of the questions is no. The first red flag is that they never make time for you. Being busy is not an excuse. Everyone is busy. If your relationship is important to them, they will make time for you regardless of their busy schedule. This is the biggest indicator that a relationship is not mutual. If you are constantly texting someone to try to get together and they are never available, then you should invest in other relationships.

If a colleague or friend is not equally invested in the relationship, they will not value or appreciate your intentionality in reaching out to them. They will not express a desire to continue the relationship because they have already shown that they are too busy to make time for you. Lastly, if someone takes all of your mental and emotional energy by talking about themselves and never has a desire to listen to what is going on in your life, that is another big sign that the relationship is not mutual. You will notice the relationship is not mutual through observing people's behaviors and actions.

Relationship List

I have made it clear that a relationship needs to be mutual, but this can look very different for each relationship and does not need to look like mutual initiation all the time. Let me share how I have been very intentional in my relationships. I have a relationship list. What is that? It's a list of everyone I want to intentionally keep in my life, regardless of where I am located and where they are located.

You might think this sounds weird, and maybe it is. But it is how I have found I can be the most intentional in friendships. It is important to note that each person's relationship list will look different. Some might have a lot of people on their relationship list, and some might have only a few. The number depends on your personality and how much you enjoy being with others. But you need to create one. Start by asking yourself the following questions.

Relationship List Questions

1. Who is most important to me? Whom do I want to keep in my life regardless of life stage we are in?
2. What friends or colleagues do I want to intentionally keep in my life regardless of where I am physically located?
3. Who do I want to have in my life forever? Who is impossible to imagine living without?

I use four categories when creating the relationship list. They are personal friends, professional friends, mentors, and people you mentor. There may be a couple of people you want to be intentional with in each category. Once you create your list, put it in a place where you will see it regularly. You get to choose how many people are on the list, how many are in each category, and how often you want to initiate with each person. These are *your* choices.

I usually initiate the most often with my closest friends and mentors. I will reach out to the rest of the people every couple of months to catch up.

That is what has worked for me. If you start to feel overwhelmed by the list you create, that is probably because there are too many people on it. Pick the people who are the most important to keep on your list—the people whom you can't imagine going through life without. Then make sure to look through the list once a week and ask yourself whom you need to reach out to and reconnect with.

CHAPTER 2
Intentional Networking

I was at a free networking event when I met a business coach. He shared that he had seminars and would love it if I attended one. We exchanged business cards, and that was the end of it—or so I thought. A week later, I received several emails from him and multiple voicemails on my phone from his assistant. She assumed I was interested in attending one of his seminars and was trying to ascertain which one I would attend. I ignored the emails and the assistant's pressure tactic. Then, as if I hadn't made my lack of interest clear enough, he called me directly. This is a common story in networking. It is why we sometimes wince when we think about networking. When networking is just meeting a bunch of people who are in it for themselves—to promote themselves—it is no fun. We quickly become tired and drained by the networking event instead of feeling energized and excited by it.

A Better Way to Network
Networking is not always enjoyable and can be hard for those of us who are not extroverts. There is a better way to approach it. The goal is to find an environment where people are *seeking mutual benefit* rather than only being in it for themselves. For me, that environment is the Lancaster (Pennsylvania) Chamber of Commerce. There are chambers of commerce all over the United States, and I have found that they are the best place to network. Beyond a chamber, any paid networking group will always be a better experience than a free networking group, because when people pay for a networking group, they are more invested in it.

When I say networking can be fun, you might wonder how that is possible. I am talking about a networking group where people have the primary goal of building relationships. My definition of networking is *building mutually beneficial relationships.* The key word in this definition is *mutual.* It is okay to utilize your network to gain opportunities, but if you are only interested in getting something from others, you will quickly find that your networking approach is unsuccessful.

In her book, *Captivate: The Science of Succeeding with People,* Vanessa Van Edwards addresses this problem and points to the reason for it. "Think you can just fake it until you make it? Think again! We can spot a fake smile a mile away. Over 4,361 people have taken our virtual Body Language Quiz to assess their nonverbal intelligence. In one question we show participants a genuine smile hidden among three fake smiles. Over 86.9% of participants are correctly able to pick out the genuine smile."[4]

So, what makes networking fun and not tiring? It is when you are networking with others who have the same purpose as you do. When both people are focused on building mutually beneficial relationships that are genuine and authentic, you will be amazed that you not only enjoy networking, but you also gain opportunities that you weren't even overtly seeking.

"Faking it until you make it is not worth the effort. Happy people make us happy, but fake happy people? They are forgettable. The first step in winning the social game is to control the situations you play in. Only interact in places where you don't have to fake it," Van Edwards writes. "No matter how many behavior hacks you learn, if you go to events that make you unhappy, it will be incredibly difficult to increase your memorability."[5]

How to Enjoy Networking

Van Edwards encourages people to find the places they enjoy being at to network. She calls these your "thrive" places. When it comes to networking, people can tell if you are trying to fake it until you make it. They can tell if you want to be there or not. So, to be genuine and authentic, you must first want to be there. The combination of this and focusing on building mutually beneficial relationships will make you successful in networking. So, find the places where you thrive, and build relationships there. If you're not sure where to start, just go to an event without a goal and focus on being present and enjoying getting to know other people. This will help you let your guard down and lean into the moment.

Questions to Ask When Networking

When identifying others we want to connect with, we should ask ourselves several questions. These questions help us find others who are also focused

---

4 Vanessa Van Edwards, *Captivate: The Science of Succeeding with People* (Penguin Random House, 2018), pp. 19–20.
5 Ibid. p. 20.

on building mutually beneficial relationships. The first question we must ask ourselves is, "Is this person professional?" This might seem obvious, but it is important because it is a filter we often use unconsciously. Being professional comes down to self-awareness. When you are self-aware and can read and observe what others are doing, you can maintain professionalism. When people lack self-awareness, this usually leads to unprofessional behavior, such as gossiping, failing to respect others' personal space, flirting, and monopolizing conversation. Examples of professionalism include giving people eye contact, listening well, asking good questions, and engaging in a dialogue back and forth.

The second question we should ask ourselves is, "Is this person interested in building a relationship with me or just trying to sell me something?" This goes back to the story I told at the beginning of this chapter. If someone acts like the business coach did, that is a clear sign that they are in it for themselves and not to build relationships. These are the people of whom you ask one question—such as, "What do you do?"—to which they give a five-minute speech about what they do that is designed to teach you something. These are not the people who want to build mutually beneficial relationships.

The last question you must ask yourself is, "Do I know and like this person enough to build trust with him or her?" You want to find other people with whom you can connect and build trust. If your answers to these three questions about new acquaintances are yes, please continue to get to know them better by asking them questions about themselves. Once you identify people looking to build relationships, the conversation will flow back and forth as you ask each other questions.

Why Business Cards Matter

At the end of the conversation, you will want to ask your new acquaintance for a business card. What is the point of connecting if you don't have any way to stay connected or contact them after the event? Sometimes, people do not have their business cards at networking events, which astounds me. I honestly cannot understand why someone would attend a networking event without their business cards. It suggests a lack of professionalism.

Here's an example. I was at a networking event once, and someone approached me and asked what I did for a living. I shared a bit about my business, and they said they were a bookkeeper. Then, this person, who was just slightly older than I was, went on to lecture me about why I needed bookkeeping as a small-business owner. I was still learning the difference between a Diminisher and an Illuminator (more on the distinction between the two in chapter 9), and so, as I always do at networking events, I asked for their card. Instead, they pulled out a printed piece of paper in the shape of a business card. I quickly left the conversation. Why? Because that bookkeeper's lack of a card struck me as unprofessional. This combined with the long-winded lecture on why I needed their services confirmed that they were mainly interested in promoting themselves and were not invested in building relationships that were mutually beneficial.

As you build relationships and find people interested in your services, having business cards with you is just common sense. That said, if you meet someone who doesn't have a card on hand but *does* seem interested in building a mutual relationship, you can do two things. You can ask them to type their name and email address on your phone in the notes section. Or if you have a piece of paper, they can write it down, which might be more manageable. Or if that sounds like too much of a bother, you can just write their name on your phone in your notes. I do this all the time. If I write down someone's name and company, I can usually find him or her on LinkedIn. People generally wear name tags bearing their names and business names at networking events, so this is easy to do.

If someone does offer a business card, take it. I always keep my phone and business cards in my left hand and put all the business cards I receive with my stack of cards to avoid losing any. Later, I put all the business cards into an organizer. This practice might sound very old school, since people sometimes want to exchange virtual business cards. But the virtual cards are not catching on. This is because if someone only saves your phone number and name, they may "lose" you in their contacts. When you're networking, you meet many people, and it can be easy to forget someone's name. Plus, people still like having paper business cards.

Never assume someone wants your business card. I usually take someone's business card and then wait for them to ask for my card if they want it. If you assume and just hand someone your business card, it can come off as though you're trying to be promotional, and that turns people off. When you print your business card, make sure it is not generic but contains your personal information. I have my name, email address, cell phone number, and website on my business cards. I also have a professional headshot of myself, my business logo, and a QR code to my LinkedIn profile.

Starting to Network
When you first start networking, it can be scary if you don't know anyone. You enter the room, and everyone is in groups, talking. After you have been networking for a while, it is easier to get pulled into groups. You will see someone you know, and they see you and say hi, and then you get pulled into that group. But when you start networking, you need to force yourself out of your comfort zone, go to a group, and join it. Even though I'm extroverted,

this was hard for me to do when I started networking, but it is a common and normal thing to do at a networking event. People do it all the time.

Another tip: if you go to an event with coworkers or people you know, hanging out with them all night can be tempting. However, the whole purpose of networking is to meet new people. So get out of your bubble, walk around, and meet new people. Sometimes, it can help to let the people with whom you attend the event know ahead of time that this is your plan. I always say hi to people I know and meet new people when I attend networking events. The wonderful thing about networking is that you can utilize these events to maintain professional relationships. Instead of meeting with everyone you know one-on-one, you can catch up at monthly networking events.

CHAPTER 3
Intentional Follow-Up

After you go to a networking event, it is vital to intentionally follow up with the people you met who were not just self-promotional. If you asked each person you met for a business card, you have their names and contact information. The first thing I do after a networking event is send each person I met a LinkedIn connection request with a personalized message. I tell them: "It was great meeting you last week at the Lancaster Chamber mixer. I look forward to connecting with you further!" Connecting with everyone you meet at a networking event on LinkedIn is the first thing you should do because it gives you an easy way to stay connected with them. It is important to note that in order to write a personalized message with each connection request you send, you will need to have a premium subscription, since LinkedIn limits the number of personalized invitations to connect you can send on free accounts. It is an investment, but it is worth it. It is also important to maintain a good LinkedIn profile that fully represents you professionally.

As mentioned in the last chapter, I have kept every business card I have been given. I recommend that you do the same. You never know when you'll need to have someone's email or phone number on hand. I use business card organizers. If you connect on LinkedIn with each person you have met at a networking event, it gives you a virtual rolodex you can reference anytime you need to reach out to someone in your network.

Choosing Whom to Connect With

It is your decision whom you follow up with and whom you do not. You cannot get together with every person you meet at a networking event, so you must create criteria for the type of people you want to connect with.

This is what I recommend. The first type of person you want to reach out to are those who express an interest in your products or services. Depending on what you do, you can connect in whatever way it works best for you—over a phone call, video call, or at an in-person meeting. When I was in college and networking, it was easy to find people who needed help with optimizing their LinkedIn profiles. When someone expressed an interest in my services, I would follow up with a phone call to share the process I would use to optimize their profile. Their response was usually a quick yes or no because they had already expressed an interest in getting help with their LinkedIn profile.

When I say to follow up or reach out to people interested in your products or services, this is not an invitation to reach out to everyone, promote what you do, and ask them if they are interested. If you do that, you will quickly find your networking efforts unsuccessful. You need to follow up *only* with those who clearly expressed an interest in what you do or said they might need your help.

The next people I connect with are those in an industry similar to mine or in the sector I eventually want to be in. This is important because you always want to build relationships with others in your industry. When you are connected to many people in other companies, you have a better chance of getting another job, shifting your career trajectory, or moving into a higher position of leadership as you advance your career.

Next, I connect with the decision-makers, executives, or high-level leaders. These people generally will not be at your networking event; their employees will go instead. If you are interested in connecting with executives, you need to find the right events to attend so you can connect with them. Larger chambers of commerce will usually have certain events that attract higher-level people.

An essential thing to know about decision-makers is that their time is very important, and it is usually hard to get a meeting with them. I have met with many executives over the years and found that when I meet them at an event, they are willing to connect afterward, but you must be willing to connect with them at their convenience, not yours. You can do this by being flexible and working around their schedule to accommodate them.

Often, executives are used to everyone wanting something from them, so they are picky about who they give their time to—and rightfully so. You must show them you are focused on building a relationship with them and learning from their experience. Leaders love to share their expertise when younger, emerging professionals are seeking guidance and wisdom instead of trying to get a job or sell them something. Executives usually have an assistant, so be willing to work through that person to schedule a meeting. And know that you often cannot stay in contact with them long-term because they are very busy.

The last category of attendees I connect with is the people who are fun. What does this mean? It can mean anything. You don't need a specific reason to connect with someone. If you meet someone at a networking event, really like them, and just want to build a relationship with them, that is totally okay. I have met some of my closest professional connections this way.

How to Connect Further

Often, when you reach out to people to connect, they ask why you want to meet or what you want to discuss. This question comes from the fact that people are used to others being in it for themselves, wanting something from them, or trying to sell something to them. I am always trying to build relationships, so my answers vary, but usually, I say I would like to get to know them better and learn from their experience. Your goal must always be building the relationship. Once people see that this is your goal, they will calm down and enjoy your meeting.

You must figure out the best form of communication when trying to connect with someone. What is the easiest way to get ahold of that person? The methods of communication I use are phone calls, emails, text messages, and direct messages on LinkedIn. When you are at a networking event, ask the people with whom you want to build relationships what the best way is to get in touch with them.

When I was in college, I would usually call someone first and then follow up by text or email. When you communicate with someone in two different ways, the chances that they will get back to you are much higher. You want to make sure you're not following up so often that you annoy them, but it is okay to use two methods of communication in one day. Then, if you are still waiting to hear back from them in a couple of days, feel free to give them another call. People are always busy and juggling multiple things, so it is essential to be understanding and not get mad if they don't respond to you right away. Try to be understanding and not make assumptions about someone if they don't respond to your communication. Now that I am working full-time, the primary way I communicate with people is through LinkedIn direct message. I have found that this is an easy way to get ahold of someone when their phone notifications are blowing up with calls, texts, and emails.

Another vital thing to do if you are trying to connect or meet with someone is to give them a choice in how you meet. I always ask people if they prefer to meet virtually or in person. While you might prefer to meet in person, some people primarily meet with others virtually, utilizing platforms like

Zoom or Teams. If you want access to someone's time, you must be flexible. How we meet people has changed so much since the Covid-19 pandemic. Video calls are a great tool for staying connected with people who live far away from you. They are also a great way to meet someone who lives locally, while also saving the time it would take to drive to and from that meeting. I prefer to meet people face-to-face, but I do meet with people over Zoom, because it saves a lot of time and many people prefer it.

When someone gives you their time, show that you are thankful. I am not always consistent in doing this, but I encourage you to email them, telling them you enjoyed the conversation and thanking them for meeting with you. While the advice in this chapter may seem obvious to some, it is important to say that follow-up is everything. It takes time and intentionality to build relationships. If a new acquaintance ignores multiple forms of communication over a couple of weeks, then that might be a sign to move on to someone else who is more interested in connecting.

Intentionally following up with people is an essential part of networking. Going to an event and meeting people is great, but those relationships only grow with intentional follow-up. If you just go to a bunch of networking events, meet a lot of people, and then move on with life without intentionally connecting further, the networking has little value. *Networking* is a term thrown around a lot in business. Unfortunately, the practice has gained a bad reputation over time because people associate negative experiences with the word. But if you can be intentional about building relationships, networking can be incredibly beneficial.

CHAPTER 4
Intentional Goals

When networking, you must go in knowing your purpose. That means knowing what your goals are. I have five.

Goal 1
Your first goal should be to build relationships. I say it many times in this book because it bears repeating. Building relationships needs to be your main goal and priority from the beginning. Without that goal, you won't be successful in any other networking goals you set for yourself.

Goal 2
The second goal is to meet people you can do business with. You want to connect with the right people to do business with—those who are interested in your products or services. This interest in what you offer could come from someone you meet directly or from someone you hear of indirectly through a referral. When you tell someone what you do, and they ask a lot of questions to get more details about your product or services, this is a sign they might be interested in potentially working with you.

Goal 3
Part of building a network is having many people who know what you do and will refer people to you when they encounter someone in need of your product or services. This leads to your third goal: building a referral network. What does this mean? It means that you know so many people that you start to find that a lot of your business comes from people you don't know, but to whom you were recommended. As you build relationships, people will like your products or services and talk about them to others. The more people I

know, the more often I get introduced by one person to another, and they share what I do. I don't need to sell what I do and its value. Someone else does it for me. This will start to happen as you build your referral network.

Goal 4

Another goal is to gain opportunities. The next chapter is completely focused on this idea. While an opportunity can mean doing business with people, it can also include many other things. For example, looking for a full-time job. If you've lost your job or just graduated from college, the best thing you can do is network. When people ask you what you do, it's easy to share that you're looking for a job—more on this in the next chapter. Networking also gives you a fantastic opportunity to share information if you have a new product or service that you want people to know about.

Goal 5

My last goal is to learn new things. The great thing about networking is that when you have networked for a while, you have a group of contacts who are great referrals and people from whom you can learn things. Building good relationships allows you to meet up with anyone in your network if you need help. And more often than not, people are happy to help you. In addition to developing a referral network, you can also be a source of referrals for others. You have all of these people you know, like, trust, and can recommend to others who are looking for help with products or services for just about any situation that may arise.

When networking and pushing yourself outside your comfort zone, set a goal for how many new people you will meet at each event. At most events I attend, it's easy to meet five new people, so that's where I set my goal. But if that sounds overwhelming to you, you can set your goal lower. At networking events, you can meet several people at a time because you join group conversations. When networking, always value quality over quantity. It's about building relationships, not just meeting people you don't connect with and getting a bunch of business cards.

Becoming an Established Networker

Another great goal you should have once you are an established networker is to become a connector of people. What does this mean? Every time you meet a new person and learn what he or she does, you should be thinking, "Who do I know who could be a beneficial connection for this person?" This is assuming, of course, that the new contact is a competent, ethical professional. Being a connector of people is something I want to get better at. I have a friend who is fantastic at this. Every time I meet with her, she is willing to connect me with people she knows who might be beneficial for me to know as well. And I try to do the same for her.

Once you are an established networker, your goals change. Networking becomes easier because you can go to any event and always run into people you know. Another goal of networking, once you're an established networker, is maintaining relationships. What do I mean by this? Whenever I am at an event and see people I know, I always try to say hi to them first. Networking is a great way to maintain relationships by quickly catching up with people you know, and that makes networking fun.

One cautionary tip I would give an established networker is that talking only to people you know is tempting, because it is easier. But you should not do this. At a two-hour networking event, you ideally will use 25 percent of your time catching up with people and 75 percent meeting new people. You need to remember that your goal is to build new relationships. At events where most people share that goal, it is easier to accomplish.

CHAPTER 5
Intentional Opportunities

Now that I have thoroughly covered various aspects of networking, it is time to talk about how you can utilize networking to gain opportunities intentionally. Now, when I say *gain opportunities*, do not hear me wrong. This does not mean that you view networking as transactional and are only concerned with what you can get from others. It means that when the goal of building intentional relationships is at the forefront, you will be surprised by how many opportunities you gain through those great relationships.

This becomes easy when you are an established networker because you have already built a network that naturally produces opportunities. But to demonstrate how you gain opportunities, I'll share my story with you so you can better understand what I am talking about.

How I Started Networking

I started networking at the end of my sophomore year in college. I began by attending an event at which I knew absolutely no one. And I mean *no one*. I learned about the event through a post on LinkedIn. So I went. Even though I am an extroverted person, this was outside of my comfort zone.

I started meeting people, and eventually, by the end of the event, I got to know many of them. At that point, I realized that it was necessary to update my LinkedIn profile, because I was actively using that platform to connect with people. So, I tried to update my profile, but it was super complicated and confusing. So, I did a lot of research on LinkedIn and improved my profile, and in the process, I realized that many people could use help in building out their profiles. Shortly thereafter, I created a website and ordered business cards. I had not planned to form my own business, but it became a fun side hustle throughout college that provided enough income to pay essential bills so I could focus more on classwork.

I started networking like crazy, going to every single event that I could find. I had yet to learn how many networking groups were out there. I went to free networking groups, paid networking groups and events, and women-in-business networking events. I would drive to networking events that were forty minutes to an hour away. The first year I had my own small business, I visited more than ten different networking groups. Eventually, I heard about the Lancaster Chamber. I didn't have any intentional goals. I simply knew that I wanted to build relationships and that this skill would be beneficial in the future for finding internships and jobs. Naturally, I gained business through those relationships because I had a professional service to offer that no one had heard of before.

Then, I attended a speed-networking event at the Lancaster Chamber of Commerce called Get Connected. The event was fast paced, and I met a lot of new people. I grew up in Lancaster, so it made sense for me to join the Lancaster Chamber. But I assumed it would cost too much. I was wrong. It was very affordable since I was a small business owner. So I joined.

From there, I was introduced to the world of chambers for networking. While I've visited many other chambers since then, I've remained a member of the Lancaster Chamber. It arranges networking events and helps members with professional development and advocacy. Every month, the chamber plans many different events that I can attend. While I primarily attend the chamber mixers, I visit other events when I can.

It makes sense to stay committed to the chamber where I live. It is a large chamber in my area, so it gives me the opportunity to do more things when it comes to attending events. As it turns out, it is also an organization whose members are focused on building relationships. In the next chapter, I'll talk about how to find the groups that add the most value and are most worthy of your time.

I've told you the story of how I began networking and continue to network to give you context for what I will share next: I began to find *many* opportunities unintentionally. As I built intentional relationships and people heard what I did, they asked about services that I was not yet offering. I ended up adding those services to my business. The primary one was building LinkedIn company pages. I started working with new clients almost every week. This was the first opportunity I gained through networking.

Then, someone asked me to speak at an event on the topic of how to create a great LinkedIn profile. I had never thought of myself as a speaker before but saw this as a great opportunity. Unbelievably, the person who gave me my first opportunity to speak was someone I'd met at my first Get Connected event at the Lancaster Chamber. He was the leader of another networking group. So, I said yes and put together a short presentation on how to create a great LinkedIn profile. After that first presentation, I was offered many other speaking opportunities.

By the age of twenty-two, I had worked with sixty-five clients and spoken at twenty different events. How did this happen? It happened through building genuine and authentic relationships. I chose to say yes to the right opportunities and no to the wrong ones, and I stayed within my specific expertise of building LinkedIn profiles.

Creating an Elevator Pitch

Gaining opportunities in networking is easier than you might think. I have done it over the years primarily by developing an "elevator pitch" to explain what I do. The pitch is so named because it should be no longer than a chat on an elevator ride. It goes something like this. "Hi, my name is Sarah Mehesy. I am the founder and owner of Impressions Matter. I write people's personal and company LinkedIn profiles, and I also speak to groups about how to optimize their LinkedIn profiles. I focus on helping you clearly communicate who you are, what you do, and why you love what you do on your LinkedIn profile. Often, people are worried about their first impression at a networking event. But they don't think about what everyone does after a networking event. They look you up on LinkedIn. I help you make a good first impression *online* through your LinkedIn profile."

My pitch describes the value of my service. People who care about having a good brand and making a good first impression online will work with me. I never offer any guarantees or metrics. But once people update their profiles, what they do and who should connect with them became obvious. When my clients stay active on LinkedIn by sharing likes, comments, and posts, those activities lead other people back to their profiles, thereby increasing the visibility of their businesses.

I don't share my entire elevator speech right away when people ask me what I do. I never want to sound promotional; I'm focused on building the relationship. When asked what I do, I share that I have my own business, Impressions Matter, where I write people's LinkedIn profiles. Then, people usually ask me more questions, and as the conversation progresses, I share more details of the pitch.

I worried at first about whether people would take me seriously because I was young. I was still in college, after all. But I found the opposite to be true. My age was an asset, not a liability.

Through my experience of starting my business, beginning to build intentional relationships, and gaining terrific opportunities that I never thought

I would have at such a young age, several things stood out to me. First, people were impressed that I had my own business and was networking at a young age. Second, people were always willing to help me and give me advice or beneficial connections with others. Third, when someone introduced me at an event, they would say that I was good at building relationships. I started hearing this over and over again, and that is why I decided to write this book. I realized that some things that seemed to come naturally to me might not be as obvious to others, and those people might be able to benefit from what I have learned.

The Power of Building Relationships

I want to emphasize that I couldn't have accomplished all these things without the support of the people I met by networking. I had to take action to step out of my comfort zone and go to networking events. I took the risk of starting my own business. But it was the people around me who propelled me to where I am today. Every single client, speaking opportunity, internship, or job opportunity has come about because of the people in my network who took a risk on me and gave me an opportunity. If you are one of those people who gave me an opportunity and are reading this book, thank you. Thank you for giving me a chance, whether you were my client, asked me to speak at your event, interviewed me for a job, or gave me your time through a meeting to learn something.

If someone was interested in being my client, they expressed interest. If someone had a speaking opportunity, they let me know about it. When I was looking for an internship in college or a job after graduation, I would share that. By simply being open and sharing what was new or currently going on in my work life, I could connect with the right opportunities.

This is how you discover opportunities. It is not that hard. When you own a business or work for someone else, please do not feel the need to be promotional or pushy to get clients. I hope my story helps you understand how to gain opportunities through networking. Opportunities are gained through building intentional relationships. That is why I stress over and over again that this is the primary focus and goal of my networking and that it should be yours, too.

Networking can be fun and enjoyable, not tiring and exhausting. It enables you to find the groups that are most worthy of your time. I will explore the time factor in the next chapter. As great as networking and visiting a ton of groups was when I started, I quickly had to cut back and figure out which networking events produced the most value for my time, money, and effort.

CHAPTER 6
Intentional Time

When you start networking, it is a good idea to visit many types of groups to discover what kind of groups you like and which are worth your time. Every event you go to takes your time, so you need to figure out which ones are worth your time and which ones are not.

To decide what networking groups you enjoy and are worthwhile, think through your networking goals. This helps determine if a networking group is worth your time. In another chapter, I talked about the different goals you can have. The main thing you want to look for in a networking group is members who are looking to build relationships, not people who only want to sell you something.

Choosing Where to Invest Your Time
As a rule of thumb, paid networking groups are usually better. This is true because people who pay for a group are invested in making the time they spend worthwhile. In my experience, free networking groups are not usually worth your time. I have attended several free networking groups and have always left feeling drained. Free groups tend to attract more people who are promoting themselves instead of being focused on building relationships.

A second type of group I visited were "closed referral groups." These are groups that are invitation-only and do not allow competitors to be part of the same group. There can only be one photographer, one plumber, one financial adviser, and so on. This is because the goal of the networking group is to get regular referrals from each other. These groups usually have regular meetings, required attendance, a high fee to join, and they require that members make referrals and track them. While I can understand the intent of these networking groups, I am not a fan of them. They tend to be transactional and not relational, and they are a bit demanding.

Another type of group that was not a great investment of time for me was young-professional events. Because there are *only* young professionals there, you will mostly connect with people who are in a stage similar to yours—there are few mentors among the attendees. However, young-professional groups can be a good way to get started if networking is scary or intimidating to you. You'll meet people your age, but beneficial connections can be limited. I have always liked general networking events and mixers because they include people who span a wide age range and are at different places in their careers.

Finding Good Networking Groups
When it comes to paid networking groups, I recommend joining a large chamber of commerce in your area. For me, that was the Lancaster Chamber. This is my favorite group to be a part of because it has enjoyable monthly mixers. Members are focused on building relationships first. They genuinely want to get to know you and don't only want to sell you something. In addition to the mixers, the Chamber holds many other types of events, such as advocacy events and professional development sessions. They also have young-professional mixers and women-in-business mixers. This allows you to network in many different ways within one organization.

Conferences provide another valuable way to network. Every industry has its own specific regional conferences. Most have keynote speakers and breakout sessions. I love conferences because they are extended events where I can network, build relationships, develop professionally, and learn.

Another factor to consider is the flow of the event. I prefer standing-only mixer events. At networking events where everyone is standing and talking in groups, you have the opportunity to meet and talk with a lot of different people. At an event where everyone is sitting at tables, the number of people you can meet is limited. However, conferences and professional development events usually allow networking time before and after the sessions.

The examples I've shared should give you a good idea of what groups are worth considering. If you are just getting into networking, visit a variety of events. Your experience might not match mine, but the groups you find to be a good fit will be worth the investment. Just remember that your primary goal needs to be finding groups where people are focused on building mutually beneficial relationships.

PART 2

Building Intentional Relationships in Life

CHAPTER 7
Having Intentional Friendships

We are often so focused on building mutually beneficial relationships with other professionals that we sometimes forget to invest in building the most important relationships of all: our personal friendships. Many of us have the idea that we are responsible for who we become. However, this isn't entirely true. Our friends help to make us who we are. In the book *Partnering*, author Jean Oelwang writes, "We spend massive amounts of time working, finding ourselves, keeping fit, and building the breadth of our connections. Yet, we invest very little effort into increasing the depth of our connections with the people who mean the most to us. We take those relationships for granted, living under the misconception that we somehow make ourselves who we are. In reality, it is the people we surround ourselves with who make us."[6]

Building Close Friendships
So why don't we spend more time investing in meaningful, deep friendships? We don't always prioritize them as highly as other things. We can get distracted by focusing on ourselves, our work, and our family relationships. While these things are important, our personal friendships greatly impact who we become. The people who make us who we are and continually invest more time with us than anyone else in our lives should be a top priority and should not be taken for granted.

To explain this better, I want to share a quote from Arthur Brooks that hit home for me at the 2024 Global Leadership Summit. Brooks, an author and a professor at Harvard, talks about the science of happiness and how the four things that create meaning in our lives are work, family, friends,

6 Jean Oelwang, *Partnering* (Optimism Press at Penguin Random House, 2022), p. xvii.

and faith. Brooks said the following when talking about building meaningful relationships:

> For leaders, everybody's useful. You come to leadership conferences and you learn how to make a good Rolodex and a good network, and that just means people are useful. Okay, fine. I have a lot of useful people in my life. But you know, the people that make me happy, the useless ones, they just love me. I'm useless to them. They're useless to me. I don't mean worthless…. Do you have enough useless people in your life, fellow leader?[7]

Having Close Friendships

Do you have enough useless people in your life? I spent the first half of this book discussing networking and building mutually beneficial relationships, and I love doing that. But now I want to pivot to personal relationships, the ones that shape us. My four closest friends are the ones who have had the greatest impact on making me who I am today and making me want to become a better person.

I know that I can share my biggest dreams and aspirations with them because they will never judge me or put me down. They are the first people I want to share exciting news with because I know they will be happy for me. I don't have to hide my excitement out of concern that they will be jealous. We cheer each other on instead of competing. When I get sad or upset about something hard, I know I can share it with them and trust them completely to keep my confidence. They understand me and are always a call away if I need them.

This kind of friendship is something we all need to have. It can be hard to come by. I want to share a story as an example of the importance of knowing someone and being known. I am always uncomfortable in social situations because I have a restrictive diet so that my asthma and acid reflux do not act up. People are constantly pressuring me to eat in social situations, and I feel badly saying, "I can't because there is nothing that I can eat." I always have to plan ahead or eat in advance; otherwise, I am stressed. I take a packed lunch to work, and if someone wants to go out to eat with me, I have to check the restaurant's menu first to make sure it includes something I can actually eat. And even if it does, I often have to personalize my order, and the server looks at me weirdly.

Around my closest friends, I am not this way. I don't have to tell them about my diet a thousand times or remind them what I can or can't have.

---

7 From Arthur Brooks's keynote address at The Global Leadership Summit 2024, August 9, 2024, in South Barrington, Illinois.

When I go to the home of one of my closest friends to have dinner, I don't have to worry about what they will cook. When my small group from church was celebrating my birthday, and it was time for the cake, which I couldn't have, they made me a fruit bowl. When I had dinner with two of my close friends for "Galentine's Day"[8] at one of their homes, they had raspberries and strawberries ready for me at dessert time, which was so thoughtful. This is what deep, meaningful friendships look like.

Friendship can be a sensitive subject sometimes, because making and keeping friends can be challenging. We can struggle with loneliness and anxiety, which makes friendship harder. How do you even make friends in the first place if you feel like you've missed the friendship deadline and are getting older? These are the questions I hope to answer in this book. So let's talk about how to make and keep friends.

---

8 Galentine's Day, celebrated on February 13, is an unofficial day for women and girls to celebrate female friendships.

CHAPTER 8
Building Intentional Friendships

At the beginning of this book, I said that you choose who stays in your life and who leaves it. Whether this happens intentionally or unintentionally is up to you. We often let people fade in and out of our lives, but we have a choice about who stays in our lives and who doesn't.

Remember, we do not always need our relationships to be fifty-fifty. The scorecard in a friendship does not need to be even in how often you initiate contact, but the friendship does need to be mutual. To know if a friendship is mutual, ask yourself the same questions I listed in chapter 1.

Mutual Relationship Questions

1. Do they intentionally make time for you despite their busy schedule?
2. Do they value your time and appreciate your intentionality in connecting with them?
3. Do they express an enjoyment and appreciation of the friendship and a desire to continue it?
4. Have you made an equal mental and emotional investment in each other?
5. Is there a mutual give and take in the friendship, in talking, listening, and giving advice?

Reasons People Don't Initiate
Sometimes people don't initiate contact in their friendships because they are struggling with their mental health or are overwhelmed with busyness. You might be thinking these are just excuses, but this is not always the case. Depending on personality, some people just don't initiate and need a friend to

reach out and engage with them. When I was getting to know one of my closest friends, who is an introvert, she really appreciated me inviting her to events with our friend group. She said that if I hadn't done this, she probably wouldn't have formed connections with others at college the way she did.

Some people are just not great at initiating and need you to be the one to reach out. Personality seems to play a significant role. Many of my friends are more introverted, and while they love being with people, their social energy gets drained quickly, which might cause them to initiate less often.

Big Friendship

The book *Big Friendship: How We Keep Each Other Close* by Aminatou Sow and Ann Friedman discusses "stretching" in a friendship. They write:

> A healthy friendship involves stretches in both directions. When you're stretching, you're both making an effort to figure out how to adapt to your differences and to the shifting shape of your bond. Just like exercise, some of this emotional stretching feels good, and some of it will make you feel like you can't take it anymore. Stretching is being challenged in a way that is both difficult and rewarding at the same time. The amount of stretching doesn't have to feel equal in every single moment—sometimes one person will require more from a friendship than the other—but over time, the give has to even out with the take.[9]

I love this idea of stretching in a friendship. At different times, each person in a friendship will have to stretch based on his or her changing circumstances. Sometimes, one person will need to stretch more than the other, depending on what you are each going through. But there must always be a give and take with stretching, like everything else. You should not continue a friendship where someone is always taking your mental and emotional energy, talking about themselves, and never listening to what is happening in your life.

The other question I want to highlight here is, "Do they make time for you?" It is okay if you are the only one initiating, but if the other person never makes time for you and is always too busy, this is a sign that the friendship might not be mutual.

How to Make Friends

So how *do* we make friends? We were created as relational beings who desire

---

9 Aminatou Sow, Ann Friedman, *Big Friendship: How We Keep Each Other Close* (Simon & Schuster, 2020), p. 91.

to belong. We want to feel seen, heard, and valued. But finding these things can be challenging. It can be really hard to make friends as an adult. If you feel like you have missed the deadline for making friends in high school or college, it can be hard to make new friends. In her book, *You Will Find Your People: How to Make Meaningful Friendships as an Adult,* Lane Moore offers ideas for making friends. Below are paraphrased versions of the tips that stood out for me:

1. Send a direct message to someone you already interact with online.
2. If you have met people through a friend, write to one of those mutual friends whom you've always felt you get along with.
3. Initiate a get-together outside of work with "that coworker you think is cool."
4. Try putting more effort into your existing friendships, even if you think they aren't giving you what you need. That may or may not be true, and making a concerted effort to connect might just improve the relationship.
5. Aim to "make/keep plans with your friends, even though sitting inside alone, watching friendships on TV, seems way better."[10]

Tip 4 really resonates with me. Putting more effort into your existing friendships can be a great way to develop deeper friendships with the people who are already in your life. Tip 5 is also a big one for me. I often make plans with friends, and then after a long day at work, I am tired and tempted to cancel. The rule that works for me is that no matter how much I want to or feel like canceling plans, I never cancel with my closest friends. Which ideas from the list that I shared from Lane Moore's book would help you the most? Think about how you could take action on one or two of these points.

10 Lane Moore, *You Will Find Your People: How to Make Meaningful Friendships as an Adult* (Harry N. Abrams, 2023), pages 9–11.

CHAPTER 9
Intentional Illumination

One thing I have always disliked when networking was talking with someone who was not relational. Because I have networked so much, I have gotten good at spotting people who are in it for themselves versus in it to build intentional relationships. This is the reason many people do not like business networking. They view it as a transactional, two-hour event where they exchange a bunch of business cards instead of an opportunity to build relationships. We should never see any relationship in our lives—business or personal—as simply transactional. While many business relationships involve transactions, people want to be seen as individuals and not just as a means to an end.

When I meet a new person, I always focus on building a relationship first. If the other person is not interested in building a relationship, I find a way to leave the conversation quickly. Over and over again, people have told me that I am good at building relationships; that that skill is what sets me apart. When I read David Brooks's statement about the difference between a Diminisher and an Illuminator, I started to understand why people always see me that way. This description applies to both personal and professional friends.

Diminishers vs. Illuminators
In his book, *How to Know a Person: The Art of Seeing Others Deeply and Being Deeply Seen*, journalist and columnist David Brooks describes the difference between a Diminisher and an Illuminator this way:

> In every crowd, there are Diminishers, and there are Illuminators. Diminishers make people feel small and unseen. They see other people as things to be used, not as persons to be befriended. They

stereotype and ignore. They are so involved with themselves that other people are just not on their radar screen. Illuminators, on the other hand, have a persistent curiosity about other people. They have been trained or have trained themselves in the craft of understanding others. They know what to look for and how to ask the right questions at the right time. They shine the brightest of their care on people and make them feel bigger, deeper, respected, lit up.[11]

Does this sound familiar to you? When I read this, everything made a lot more sense. This applies to both our personal and professional relationships. We often experience someone who wants to meet us and use us to get to where they want to go. They ask you specific questions to see what you can do for them. We see this all too often in networking situations, but it holds true in personal relationships, too. Knowing how to identify Diminishers will help us quickly leave a conversation or remove them from our lives.

Who Are Diminishers?

In a personal context, a Diminisher uses you to get something he or she wants. Here's a story to give you an example. In elementary school, we had a book fair every year at which we could buy books. I would bring "a lot of money" to buy many books each year. It was not that much in reality, but to young elementary-school students, $40 was a lot of money. Suddenly, the kids who hated me and were always snarky to me became my "best friends." They would grab books for me and suggest what I should get. After I selected the books I was going to buy, they would ask me for money, which they promised to pay back. Obviously, I didn't give them any money because I knew they weren't being sincere. This is a funny example of a Diminisher, but it works to make my point. A Diminisher will be nice to you until they get what they want, and then they will forget you.

Whenever I meet a Diminisher at a networking event, they always hand me their business card *without me asking for one*. They are the ones I dread giving my card to, because the next day, I invariably have a promotional email in my inbox, I get called or texted, and I am added to their email list without even being asked. Diminishers are at the event to promote themselves and use people to get to where they want to go, whether that is to gain business or to get connected to a person they want to reach.

Who Are Illuminators?

Illuminators, on the other hand, genuinely desire to get to know each person

---

11 David Brooks, *How to Know a Person: The Art of Seeing Others Deeply and Being Deeply Seen.* (Random House, 2023), pages 12–13.

they come in contact with. They are curious, ask questions, and the conversation flows easily. Illuminators are people we love to build relationships with and stay connected to. This is the kind of person we should all strive to be. When I asked my dad why people keep telling me I'm good at building relationships, he said it was because I show a genuine desire to get to know other people. I realized that I am good at building relationships because I am a natural Illuminator.

In a personal setting, my closest friends, whom I met in college, are Illuminators. I always have so much fun around them. When we are one-on-one, we mutually invest in each other's lives and ask one another good questions. We want to be updated on what is happening in each other's lives. In a group setting, I have never laughed harder than I do when I am with them. We always find a way to laugh without even trying. Whether it is a funny story or something funny that happens in the moment, we laugh so hard that we cry. Sometimes, having water or food in our mouths makes us laugh harder as we attempt not to spray it all over the place.

Illuminators are curious about others, want to understand others, and know how to ask the right questions at the right time. This perfectly describes my college friends. They make others feel bigger, deeper, respected, and, yes, "lit up," as Brooks would say. Every time I leave my friends, this is exactly how I feel. We always have a fantastic time together, and I am always excited to make plans with them. When we were in college, I would plan weekends at my house for the group every semester, just to get off campus. We have always prioritized spending time together as a group and still do to this day. Now, we get together at each other's houses and apartments locally, and for those farther away, we plan weekend visits.

An example of an Illuminator in my professional life is one of my good friends and professional connections. She is always curious about what is new in my life and how she can help me. She offers to connect me with anyone she knows who it would be beneficial for me to meet and is always open to meeting with me. She intentionally connects people she thinks would benefit from meeting one another. We met at a Lancaster Chamber mixer and have been good friends ever since. She is curious and asks good questions. We have built a good relationship, and we both work to help one another in our careers in any way we can. When two Illuminators work together, they can help one another and lift each other up.

Seek to Be an Illuminator

As we seek to build relationships in business and life, we should work toward being Illuminators and not Diminishers. While we have probably all played both roles at different times in our lives, now that we understand the difference, we should always seek to be Illuminators. When we are Illuminators, we look to build genuine and authentic connections with each person we meet. We want to invest in people for the long term and want the best for them regardless of our own personal circumstances.

Being an Illuminator as you seek to build personal friendships will help you significantly. Displaying a genuine interest in others and asking questions makes it easier to build close friendships quickly. In a networking context, being an Illuminator will make you stand out in a big way because so many people at networking events are Diminishers. People will be drawn to getting to know you better. When networking, if you ignore the Diminishers and look to build intentional relationships with other Illuminators, networking will be much more fun. You will build many mutually beneficial relationships that will benefit you both personally and professionally.

So be an Illuminator, not a Diminisher. Watch out for Diminishers who pretend to be Illuminators. Build intentional relationships with others who are curious and ask conversation-stimulating questions. And be curious and ask good questions yourself. This will transform every relationship you have, both personally and professionally. This is how you build amazing relationships in business and life.

CHAPTER 10

Intentional Connection

So far, I have been talking about building intentional relationships in business and life. But I have not addressed the problem that may be lingering in your mind. We are a country and society plagued with incredibly high rates of loneliness, anxiety, and depression. This is a direct result of people not having good relationships. I don't need to quote all the statistics about this. We all know it. We hear about it every day.

Hyperindividualism

In her book *Partnering*, Jean Oelwang, president and CEO of Virgin Unite, the independent, charitable, arm of the Virgin Group, describes what she believes is causing this epidemic. She writes, "I believe the glorification of hyperindividualism has plunged us into a crisis of loneliness. We fear differences instead of celebrating them. We respond to leadership through domination rather than cooperation. We forget basic civility."[12]

Oelwang is correct. The United States has become a culture where we are individuals instead of communities. We are so focused on ourselves, our goals, and our ambitions, and we forget that the most important thing in our lives are our relationships with others. Let's face it. Without relationships, life would be lonely and boring. We were created to be in relationships with other people. I fully believe that our relationships with other people should be the most important priority in our lives.

Disconnection

David Brooks puts it this way: "We live in an environment in which political

---

12 Jean Oelwang, Partnering: Forge the Deep Connections that Make Things Happen (Optimism Press, 2022), p. xiv.

animosities, technological dehumanization, and social breakdown undermine the connection, strain friendships, erase intimacy, and foster distrust. We're living in the middle of some sort of vast emotional, relational, and spiritual crisis. It is as if people across society have lost the ability to see and understand one another, thus producing a culture that can be brutalizing and isolating."[13]

We live in a world where there is more disagreement and distrust than there is unity and trust. People are isolated and lonely and do not have meaningful relationships. Between the glorification of hyperindividualism and disconnection due to technology and political disagreements, people have a lot of broken relationships. Having deep conversations that reveal common interests, having people's backs in the sense that you help them reach their goals, and knowing that they will reciprocate will help you to reverse that trend in your life. This is why I am so passionate about building intentional relationships: it can reduce the loneliness, depression, and anxiety that so many people in our culture struggle with.

Friendship as the Ultimate Bio Hack

In an interview with Dr. Mark Hyman, a prominent advocate of taking a holistic approach to health, for his podcast "A Bit of Optimism," Simon Sinek puts it perfectly. In light of "the rising rates of anxiety and depression and mental fitness challenges and inability to cope with stress and then the worst case, suicide, [and] even the obsession with longevity…friendship is the ultimate bio hack. It is. Friendship literally fixes all of those things. We know the data that people who have close relationships live longer. People who have close relationships are happier."[14]

This is why the relationships we have in our lives should be the most important thing to us. Without meaningful relationships, life is not fun; it is boring and lonely. So, we want to go against the norm. Instead of being hyperindividualistic and socially disconnected, we should strive to build strong relationships and have an intentional community.

To go against the norm, you need to know what to look for in current and future friendships. So, I will share with you what makes my friendships deep and meaningful. Without exception, the following statements are true.

1. I feel completely comfortable being myself around my friends.
2. I trust them completely, knowing they will keep my confidences.
3. I feel safe to tell them anything, without fear of judgment.

---

13 Brooks, *How to Know a Person*, p. 97.
14 Simon Sinek interview with Dr. Mark Hyman on the topic "To Live Longer You Need…", *A Bit of Optimism* podcast, episode 151. https://simonsinek.com/podcast/episodes/dr-mark-hyman-to-live-longer-you-need/.

4. I can share my biggest dreams with them and be encouraged instead of being put down.
5. I can share exciting news with them, and they get excited with and for me.
6. I can call them, crying or upset about something, and they will listen.

Examples of Deep & Meaningful Friendship

I feel completely comfortable being myself around my closest friends because they have seen me at my best and my worst. I am honest with them when they ask me how I am doing. It is important that you have people in your life with whom you can answer that question honestly and who really want to hear your honest answer.

I never hesitate to share what is going on in my life because I know I can trust them. We have built a close trust through our years of friendship. Trust is not something we have instantly; it takes time to build. Even if we have the desire to be open and vulnerable, it still takes time to build trust with other people so we can get to the point where we are completely open and vulnerable. This is why it is so important to take the time to invest in our relationships.

I feel safe to tell my friends anything, without fear of judgment. This comes from the trust we've built by getting to know each other's stories. We both know the tough things the other has been through and what we are each facing currently. We both know our regrets and mistakes, allowing us to have a mutual understanding and a feeling of safety in our conversations.

I can and do share my biggest dreams with my friends, knowing they will be encouraging and not put me down. It is with my closest friends that I have shared my dream to write this book. It is my hope that this book will have an impact on many people. Helping people build intentional relationships is my *why* in life. It is my passion. My friends have never put me down for this dream. They have always encouraged me and gotten excited for me. Do you have people in your life with whom you feel comfortable voicing your biggest dreams, knowing they will encourage you?

I can also share exciting news with my friends, and they become excited with me. I don't need to worry about them getting jealous, because I know they will share in my joy and excitement. Being the friend that someone wants to tell exciting news to is important.

A Closer Level of Friendship

Sinek calls this "a closer level of friendship." He describes it as "when you can call somebody when something amazing happens. And they're not jealous. And there's no jealousy. And you can call them. And what you're doing is bragging, but not really. You just need to tell someone about this amazing thing that you accomplished, or that was given to you, or that was won or whatever it is. And if you told anyone else, they'd think you're bragging. But to *that* friend, they have unbridled joy with you and for you. And what I've learned is the number of people I would call with good news is actually smaller than the number of people I would call with bad news."[15]

To call people with good news, you need to know that they will celebrate with you and not be jealous. Lastly, you need to know that your friends are one quick call away if something hard is going on, or if you need to mentally process something with them. My closest friends are the ones I call when something happens that I need to talk through. It is essential you have people you can call when you need to clarify your own thoughts.

In describing my friends here, I have talked from personal experience about the six things that make my friendships deep and meaningful. These are the things you should look for in a friendship. But I also encourage you to be this kind of friend to others. Friendship is a two-way street, and you need to have a mutual investment in each other for a friendship to work well.

---

15 Sinek, *A Bit of Optimism*, episode 151.

CHAPTER 11
Intentional Belonging

Each one of us is hardwired for connection and belonging. We were created with the desire to be in relationships with other people and to be in a community. In the previous chapter, I talked about how the struggles of loneliness, anxiety, and depression are a direct result of a lack of meaningful relationships in our lives. Building intentional relationships solves a lot of these issues because when we have meaningful relationships, we have people we can reach out to for help in our struggle. However, I did not address the fact that building good relationships can be very hard because we have never been taught this skill in life. Brooks addresses this difficulty:

> The real act of, say, building a friendship or creating a community involves performing a series of small, concrete social actions well: disagreeing without poisoning the relationship; revealing vulnerability at the appropriate pace; being a good listener; knowing how to end a conversation gracefully; knowing how to ask for and offer forgiveness; knowing how to let someone down without breaking their heart; knowing how to sit with someone who is suffering; knowing how to host a gathering where everyone feels embraced; knowing how to see things from another point of view. These are some of the most important skills a human being can possess, and yet we don't teach them in school. Some days it seems like we have intentionally built a society that gives people little guidance on how to perform the most important activities of life. As a result, a lot of us are lonely and we lack deep friendships. It's not because we don't want these things. Above almost any other need, human beings long to have another person look into their face with loving respect and acceptance.

It's that we lack practical knowledge about how to give each other the kind of rich attention we desire.[16]

My Story

Since we are often not taught the skills required to build good relationships, many of us struggle to build genuine and authentic connections with others, and that can result in the struggles we have with loneliness. When I was born, the umbilical cord was wrapped around my neck, resulting in a loss of oxygen. This caused me to have major speech problems that were so bad that even my parents could not understand me. As I was growing up, my mom hauled me and my siblings around for my speech therapy, tutoring, and physical therapy. When I got tired of it all, she set up a special time for me to have lunch with my speech therapist and paint her nails.

My parents never knew if I could get past my struggles to succeed in school and life. During my first couple of years in public school, I was bullied pretty hard. One time, for example, I helped make the birthday cupcakes that my friend brought for our class. But when I mentioned that I'd helped to bake them, no one would eat them. Throughout my entire school and college career, I have never been great at academics. Along the way, people said I should use my struggles as an excuse to be evaluated by lower standards than everyone else had.

I never allowed myself to use my extra struggles as an excuse. In school, I struggled with memorization and information retention. I still struggle with that to this day. When I was bullied, I struggled to make good friendships. School became a place where I was trying to survive instead of thriving. What enabled me to start doing better was making friends. I started by building relationships with people who had no friends. These were often kids who had autism. They were incredibly kind but struggled to learn how to communicate with others effectively. As a result, they didn't have friends, and they were also bullied. What I learned by befriending these kids is that they had something of value to offer that most people didn't see because they were dismissive of them or avoided them all together.

I share my story to help you understand that I know what it is like to struggle to build good relationships. I feel very blessed to be where I am today and to have built the kind of meaningful and deep relationships I have. I hope that every single person reading this book can have amazing relationships as well.

If you were not taught friendship-building skills when you were growing up or are considered "different," you may have been put down instead of celebrated for your differences. I encourage you to have patience as you are

---

trying to build good relationships, because a lot of people struggle with the social skills needed for relationships. We are not taught the most basic skills required to be successful. Because this is true, we fumble around trying to learn these skills.

Whom to Share Your Story With

It can be hard to know whom to trust and invest in. How do we know whom to share with, what to share, and when? In her book, *The Gifts of Imperfection*, Brené Brown writes, "We have to own our story and share it with someone who has earned the right to hear it, someone with whom we can count on to respond with compassion."[17] Ask yourself, "Has this person earned the right to hear my story?" This question can save us a lot of pain and heartache.

At the beginning of this chapter, I talked about how we have all been hard-wired and created with the desire for connection and belonging. But to understand how to get these things, we must first understand what they mean. It can be very easy to throw around words in our culture and say this or that is important. But we must define our terms to know we are talking about the same thing. Brown contends that we should only share our story with someone who has earned the right to hear it and will respond with compassion. So, how do we know if someone is responding with actual compassion?

Defining Compassion, Connection, and Belonging

Brown defines *compassion* as feeling "totally exposed and completely loved and accepted at the same time,"[18] So, we should look for people who are strong enough to respond with compassion when deciding whom to share our stories with.

She defines *connection* as "the energy that exists between people when they feel seen, heard and valued; when they can give and receive without judgment; and when derive sustenance and strength from the relationship."[19] We must have people in our lives who make us feel seen, heard, and valued.

She defines *belonging* as "the innate human desire to be a part of something larger than us. Because this yearning is so primal, we often try to acquire it by fitting in and by seeking approval, which are not only hollow substitutes for belonging, but often barriers to it. Because true belonging only happens when we present our authentic, imperfect selves to the world, our sense of belonging can never be greater than our level of self-acceptance."[20]

I am sharing these definitions so you understand what to look for in current and future friendships. We often mistake being able to change ourselves

---

17 Brené Brown, *The Gifts of Imperfection*, p. 14.
18 Brown, *The Gifts of Imperfection*, p. 19.
19 Brown, *The Gifts of Imperfection*, p. 29.
20 Brown, *The Gifts of Imperfection*, p. 37.

to fit in for belonging. We mistake "anyone who will listen" for evidence that person is compassionate, and we don't pay attention to some of the rude ways people respond to us. And we mistake a link with any person we know for connection, even if we don't feel valued and accepted by that person. I feel connection, belonging, and compassion from my closest friends.

One time, I was hanging out with two of my friends for Galentine's Day. We had an amazing time, talking and laughing. We could all be completely honest with each other about where we were in life in a judgment-free zone. For the first time, I shared information about situations in which I was thriving and excited and, more crucially, those important areas in which I felt I was personally failing. I shared the unhealthy patterns I found myself getting into, and so did my friends. We shared some of the frustrations we had in other hard relationships in our lives. Making ourselves vulnerable to each other produced an amazing feeling of raw honesty. We felt completely comfortable being ourselves and sharing where we were in our lives.

I felt completely exposed and loved and accepted, all at the same time, which is compassion. I felt seen, heard, valued, and received without judgment, which is the definition of connection. And I felt like I was a part of something bigger than myself, which is belonging. Finding compassion, connection, and belonging can be hard. And even when we find it, it can take a long time to build the trust needed to feel it. But once you have found it, you will feel so safe. So look for friendships where you experience connection, compassion, and belonging.

CHAPTER 12

Intentional Big Friendship

In the busyness of life, friendship can be hard. Finding time to invest in other people can be challenging when we have work obligations and other responsibilities. We all have limited time and energy. I completely understand this feeling. When I was in college, life was busy, but I still had time during the day to meet with people. Once I started working my first full-time job, figuring out how I would intentionally invest time in all the relationships I was actively maintaining seemed like an overwhelming task. This is why we need to select who we are going to keep in our lives and who we are going to let go.

Choosing the Keepers

I know it can sound awful to remove someone from our lives, but there is only so much time in a day. We must be picky about whom to give our time to, especially those we hang out with after work. It also helps to determine how often we want to meet with each person. I have four close friends I keep in touch with every month. I connect with everyone else every couple of months. I also stay in touch with people through phone and video calls for those who don't live close to me.

You get to decide who you give your time to, and who stays in your life. As I talk about friendship, I want to acknowledge that in the craziness of life, it can be hard to be intentional in maintaining friends. But it is one of the most important things we can do. Being intentional in our relationships with others can sound hard, challenging, and even impossible, depending on your life, work, and mental health. But you will never regret investing your time with people. Not only does it improve your mental health, but it will also energize you to keep going.

Another thing that can be challenging about friendship is that everyone puts it on the back burner. People put family and romantic relationships above their friends all the time. This can become frustrating for those of us who are trying to build intentional relationships. People will drop friends when they get busy and then try to pick them up when they feel like they have more time without thinking there is any problem.

In their book *Big Friendship*, Aminatou Sow and Ann Friedman write, "We give relationships meaning by the amount of attention and work we put into them. Just as we can choose to leave our friendships unattended and hope they stay warm, we can also choose to elevate our most important friendships to a status equal to marriage, family, and career. We can choose to keep them active, to keep investing in them."[21]

Please don't get me wrong; I completely understand that people's spouses and kids have to come first in their lives most of the time. But the point I want to make is that friendships often get the short end of the stick. We don't make them one of the most important relationships in our lives. We drop in and out of friendships as life gets busy. What I propose is that we work hard to make friendships as important as the other relationships in our lives. I would encourage you to reexamine how you think about friendship. Make it a priority regardless of what is going on in your life.

In *You Will Find Your People,* Lane Moore writes:

There is so much about forming friendships that is akin to romantic relationships, even though we love to separate them, as though friendship is easy and innate, and romantic relationships are complex and daunting. But trying to get the courage to slide someone a sheet of paper that says "Do you want to be my friend? Check yes or no" across the table is no less terrifying than asking a romantic partner "What are we? Because I would like to be together." It requires the same risk, the same courage, the same hopefulness that it will work out and we will be accepted. There's no cheat code for it, or I would've found one, trust me. We just have to jump and hope they catch us.[22]

Is this how you view your friendships? I fully believe in the importance of investing in friendships, because being intentional with my friendships has changed my life for the better. We never get over the desire to have friends. Whether we are single, married, or have kids, we all still need meaningful friendships. As you start to rethink how you view friendship, I hope this discussion gives it a higher level of importance in your mind.

21 Sow and Friedman, *Big Friendship*, p. 198.
22 Lane Moore, *You Will Find Your People*, pages 31–32.

Long-Distance Friendships

I want to share an example from Aminatou Sow and Ann Friedman's book, *Big Friendship*. These two women have remained close friends throughout their whole lives, even when they worked in different parts of the country. Their friendship was often long distance.

Two of my closest friends are long distance. They have gotten married and moved away. But when we have meaningful friendships, we should continue to invest in them regardless of where we are located. Don't get me wrong; we need friends with whom we can connect in person. But I encourage you to stay invested and connected to your existing deep friendships, even if those people are not geographically close to you. FaceTime or call them. Visit them once a year to see where they live and what they are up to.

Back to Sow and Friedman's long-distance friendship. They began a podcast together to share the journey and story of their friendship. Eventually, however, they realized through a series of miscommunications that they were not as close as they used to be. They stopped being able to share the hard things that were going on in their lives and they began to inadvertently hurt each other's feelings. But they had a business together and still cared about their friendship, so they decided to spend time together in person. They went on a spa getaway together to try to rekindle their friendship. But they both went home feeling like nothing had changed between them and their walls were still up, so they decided to go to therapy. Going to therapy saved their friendship because it gave them the space they needed to talk through their struggles together and learn how to deal with those struggles.[23] While this might sound over the top and crazy to you, I don't think it is. Again, I want to encourage you to rethink where friendships fall on your priority list.

Friendships can be as meaningful as other relationships in your life that you consider to be more important. And a friendship breakup can be as painful as a romantic breakup. Friendship can be challenging. Taking the emotional risk of being vulnerable and opening up to someone can be hard. But once someone has built trust with you and earned the right to hear your story, it is worth the risk of vulnerability. Having a friend you feel completely safe with, telling the truth, and not being judged is so important. I hope this chapter has helped you rethink how you view friendship and its importance in your daily life.

---

23 Aminatou Sow and Ann Friedman, *Big Friendship*.

CHAPTER 13

Intentional Gratitude

In *The Gifts of Imperfection*, Brown quotes author and spiritual leader Marianne Williamson on the topic of joy. "Joy is what happens to us when we allow ourselves to recognize how good things really are."[24] I encourage you to do the same. What a revelation it is to discover that it is within your power to shift the way you view and approach friendships. It is within your power to experience joy.

Never take your deep and meaningful friendships for granted. Regularly reflect on how blessed you are that they have been brought into your life. Be grateful for the presence in your life of every person you value. That will allow you to truly appreciate them.

After spending time hanging out with a friend, I will walk back to my car, reflecting on how grateful I am that they came into my life. I was blessed in college to build an amazing group of friends with whom I still keep in touch to this day. I had friends growing up, but it was not until college that I built my deep friendships. I think about how it only took one invitation to a game night during my freshman year of college to meet my lifelong friends. And for that, I am so thankful.

Put It in Writing

I encourage you to write thank-you notes that tell people how they have had an impact on your life. I need to be better at writing these for my friends, but whenever I have had a major season-of-life change, such as high school and college graduation, I have written thank-you cards to the mentors who have had an impact on my life. It is important to tell people how much you appreciate their presence in your life and their guidance. Let your friends and mentors know how much they mean to you.

---

24 Brown, *The Gifts of Imperfection*, p. 111.

Lastly, I want to share a concept called "Shine Theory," a term coined by Aminatou Sow and Ann Friedman. They write:

> We came to define Shine Theory as an investment, over the long term, in helping a friend be their best—and relying on their help in return. It is a conscious decision to bring our full selves to our friendships and to not let insecurity or envy ravage them. It's a practice of cultivating a spirit of genuine happiness and excitement when our friends are doing well and being there for them when they aren't.[25]

Sow and Friedman say Shine Theory starts with refusing to give in to competition or comparison. It applies to both business and personal connections. Our goal in building friendships and networking should be to partner and collaborate with people. It should be to invest in others and help them along on their journeys—sharing knowledge and insights to help others succeed. We shine when we help others to shine. They shine by reciprocating. I encourage you to partner and collaborate with friends in business and life and help them shine.

25 Aminatou Sow and Ann Friedman, *Big Friendship*, p. 70.

Afterword

I hope that this book will enable you to build intentional relationships in business and life. Without relationships, life is boring and not fun. The intentional and meaningful relationships we form give our lives meaning and purpose. Think about that for a second: We were created to be in relationships with others. Therefore, the relationships in our lives should be among the most important things to us.

In business, networking to build intentional relationships has so many benefits. I encourage you to write out some of your networking goals and to start thinking through what it looks like to achieve them. Figure out what networking groups are worth your time and what environments you thrive in. Then have fun networking and focus on being present with each person you meet. Find a person you connect with and enjoy getting to know them without any agenda.

In life, we build some of our most meaningful relationships with close friends. We turn to these people when we have exciting news and hard news. I hope I have reshaped the way you view your business network and your personal friendships. I hope fostering friendships has risen in importance your mind. Friendships are some of the most meaningful relationships we will ever have. We should invest in them for the long term because good friends make us better people.

In this book, I have separated the relationships we have in business from those we form elsewhere. You could call them professional versus personal connections. But in reality, things are not always this separate. It is entirely okay for a professional friend to become a personal friend. Being honest and open and talking about your personal life with professional friends is okay. While the two groups are mostly separate in my life and do not often mix, I still talk about my personal life with professional friends. I love professional friends because we understand each other's excitement about professional accomplishments in a way that personal friends do not always understand.

I also want to acknowledge that the intentional relationships we build in business and our personal lives will look different as the circumstances of our lives evolve. Whether we are single, married, or a stay-at-home parent, for instance, influences the amount of energy and time we have to invest in friendships. Sometimes our levels don't match those of close friends. And that is totally okay. Being intentional in all our relationships is important, but we must also give ourselves grace. Life happens, and sometimes, things get missed. Working toward being intentional in relationships is a lifelong endeavor and pursuit. It is something we are constantly improving.

Bibliography

Brooks, Arthur. *The Global Leadership Summit.* The Global Leadership Network, 2024.

Brooks, David. *How to Know a Person.* Penguin Random House, 2023.

Brown, Brené. *The Gifts of Imperfection.* Hazelden Publishing, 2010.

Guidara, Will. *Unreasonable Hospitality.* Optimism Press at Penguin Random House, 2022.

Moore, Lane. *You Will Find Your People: How to Make Meaningful Friendships as an Adult.* Abrams Image, 2023.

Oelwang, Jean. *Partnering.* Optimism Press at Penguin Random House, 2022.

Sinek, Simon. Interview with Dr. Mark Hyman on the topic "To Live Longer You Need…" *A Bit of Optimism* podcast, episode 151, 2024. Audio. https://simonsinek.com/podcast/episodes/dr-mark-hyman-to-live-longer-you-need/.

Sow, Aminatou and Ann Friedman. *Big Friendship: How We Keep Each Other Close.* Simon & Schuster Paperbacks, 2021.

Van Edwards, Vanessa. *Captivate: The Science of Succeeding with People.* Penguin Random House, 2018.

www.ingramcontent.com/pod-product-compliance
Lightning Source LLC
Chambersburg PA
CBHW070938120626
46546CB00004B/1468